Count Your Way through

Japan

by Jim Haskins

illustrations by Martin Skoro

Carolrhoda Books, Inc./Minneapolis

To Elisa Beth and the future

This book is available in two editions:
Library binding by Carolrhoda Books, Inc.,
  a division of Lerner Publishing Group
Soft cover by First Avenue Editions,
  an imprint of Lerner Publishing Group
241 First Avenue North
Minneapolis, MN 55401 U.S.A.

Website address: www.lernerbooks.com

Library of Congress Cataloging-in-Publication Data

Haskins, James, 1941–
  Count your way through Japan.

  Summary: Presents the numbers one to ten in
Japanese, using each number to introduce concepts
about Japan and its culture.
  1. Japan—Civilization—Juvenile literature.
2. Counting—Juvenile literature. [1. Japan.
2. Counting.] I. Skoro, Martin, ill. II. Title.
DS821.H349 1987   952   87-6398
ISBN 0-87614-301-X (lib. bdg. : alk. paper)
ISBN 0-87614-485-7 (pbk. : alk. paper)

Manufactured in the United States of America
  17 18 19 20 21 – JR – 08 07 06 05 04

Introductory Note

Written Japanese is derived from written Chinese, and like Chinese it has no alphabet. Written Japanese uses some Chinese characters in combination with a uniquely Japanese system of writing symbols. A single character often forms a whole word, and a well-educated person knows thousands of characters.

Spoken Japanese is based on speech that developed in Japan long before writing was introduced there and so does not sound at all like Chinese.

The Japanese number system is also derived from Chinese. Numbers above ten are all Chinese derivations. For the numbers one to ten, the Japanese have two sets of numbers: one set is based on the Chinese numbers and the second is a Japanese counting system. The characters used to represent the numbers one to ten are basically the same for both number systems.

Numbers derived from Chinese are used when talking about people, time, months, telephone numbers, addresses, and money. The Japanese numbers one to ten can be used to speak of age or a quantity of objects.

You will be counting your way through Japan using the numbers of Chinese derivation, those most often used in Japanese conversation.

1 ー (ee-chee)

There is only **one** Fujiyama, a volcanic mountain better known to Americans as Mount Fuji. It is the highest mountain in Japan and is the most often painted and photographed landmark in that country. Mount Fuji is a dormant volcano, which means that it has not erupted in a long time. In fact, the last time it erupted was in 1707. Mount Fuji is surrounded by five small lakes, one of which is noted for its reflection of the snow-capped mountain on its still waters. Most Japanese people regard Mount Fuji as sacred, and thousands climb to the shrine at its peak every summer.

2  (nee)

Two chopsticks are the traditional Japanese eating utensils. Usually made from bamboo or wood, each chopstick is about as thick as a pencil where it is held and thinner where the stick touches the food. Chopsticks are held in one hand and are used by moving the top stick up and down while the bottom stick remains stable. Japanese children are taught how to use chopsticks when they are quite young.

3 三 (sahn)

Every Japanese person learns early in life that there are **three** things to fear in nature—earthquakes, fire, and typhoons.

The Japanese islands were formed when forces of the earth pushed them up from the ocean floor. These same forces continue to affect the islands by causing as many as 1,500 earthquakes each year.

Fires may burn out of control in the destruction following a severe earthquake. Flames used for everyday cooking and heating can ignite falling timbers as well as gas that has escaped from broken gas pipes, spreading fire quickly throughout a town.

A typhoon is a western Pacific storm. These storms' heavy rains and strong winds cause much damage across the Japanese islands, mostly during the months from July to October.

4 四 (shee)

There are **four** seasons in a year. The seasons and other cycles of nature have a great influence on Japanese culture. When the season changes, *kimonos* (kih-MO-nuhz) (traditional, robelike pieces of clothing) often reflect this change. In the summer, a person might wear a *kimono* showing a pattern of morning glories. In the fall, the robe could display chrysanthemums or maple leaves. A winter *kimono* is sometimes made of material with a snowflake pattern, and early flowers might decorate a *kimono* in the spring. In this way, Japanese people can wear the same patterns that decorate nature.

5 五 (go)

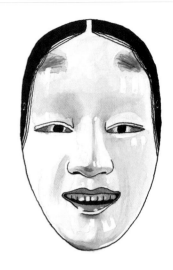

The *No* play is the oldest form of traditional Japanese theater. Japanese *No* theater combines words, music, and dance to tell stories about Japanese history and legend. *No* theater uses very few characters, and traditionally all the actors are men. There are **five** main categories of Japanese *No* plays:

(1) god plays *(Kami-mono)*

(2) battle plays *(Shura-mono)*

(3) stories of beautiful women *(Katsura-mono* Katsura means wig; since all the actors are men, naturally whoever plays a woman has to wear a wig!)

(4) present-day plays *(Genzai-mono)*

(5) and devil plays *(Oni-mono)*

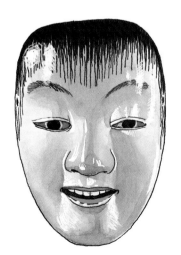

6 六 (ro-koo)

There are **six** major *sumo* (SOO-mo) tournaments in Japan each year. *Sumo*, a Japanese form of wrestling, is a very popular spectator sport in Japan. The wrestlers are large men who weigh hundreds of pounds. In a *sumo* match, the wrestlers try to throw each other down to the ground. The average *sumo* match lasts only ten seconds, so there are many matches in each tournament.

7 七 (shee-chee)

Calligraphy, writing with a brush and ink, is a fine art in Japan. There are about 1,850 written characters in common use that combine to make up the Japanese language. These characters are often divided up according to how many brush strokes it takes to make them.

The character for the words "how many" requires **seven** strokes.

How many 何

ノ イ イ イ 仁 何 何 何

8 ハ (hah-chee)

Japan is divided into **eight** major geographic regions. Three of them, Hokkaido, Shikoku, and Kyushu are located on the islands of the same name and include the surrounding offshore islands. The remaining five regions, Tohoku, Kanto, Chubu, Kinki, and Chugoku are all on the island of Honshu. Honshu is the largest of the four main islands in the group of islands that makes up Japan.

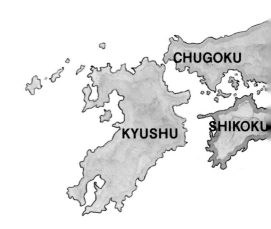

CHUGOKU

SHIKOKU

KYUSHU

9 九 (koo)

In a traditional Japanese marriage ceremony, **nine** cups of rice wine are drunk, one right after another. The cups are very small and hold only about a thimbleful of wine. Japanese rice wine is called *sake* (SAHK-ee)

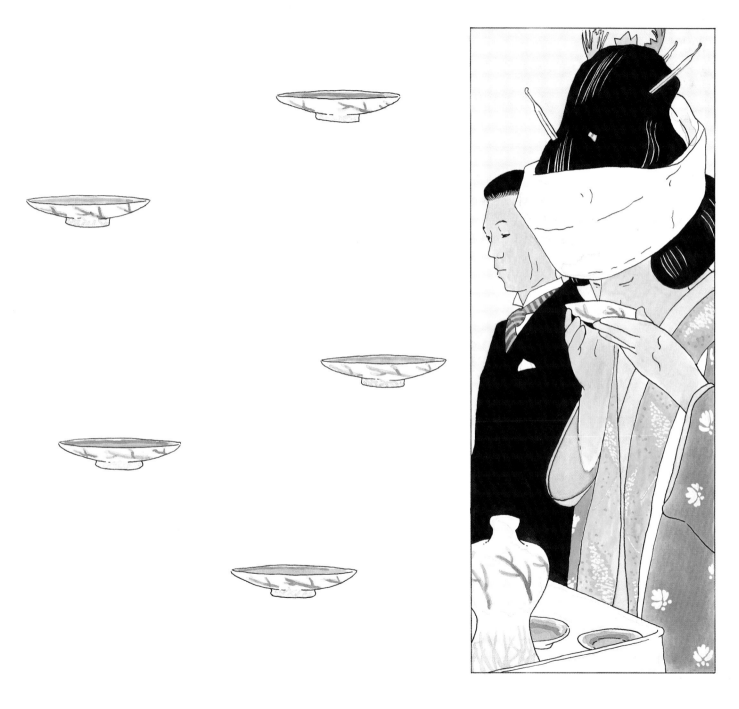

10 十 (joo)

Until they reach the age of **ten**, Japanese children are given special privileges. At age ten, however, a child must begin to take on new responsibilities. By that age, he or she is expected to start practicing to be an adult.

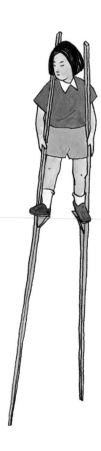

Pronunciation Guide

1 / 一 / ee-chee

2 / 二 / nee

3 / 三 / sahn

4 / 四 / shee

5 / 五 / go

6 / 六 / ro-koo

7 / 七 / shee-chee

8 / 八 / hah-chee

9 / 九 / koo

10 / 十 / joo